Winter 2008-2009
To Aunt Margaret...
to one quilt lover
from another !
& Kay

ANNA GROSSNICKLE HINES

Winter Lights

A SEASON IN POEMS & QUILTS

Greenwillow Books, *An Imprint of* HarperCollins*Publishers*

Star Catcher

Overnight
an icicle grew,
catching the stars
above my window.
Now
in the sunlight
it

sets

them

free.

Holiday Magic

My street is dull
and plain by day,
but magic comes at night.

Beaming from lampposts,
streaming through windows.
Blinking on porches,
twinkling on rooftops.

Glinting from stars,
gleaming from candles,
glittering on evergreens,
snowmen, and Santas.

Luminous! Lustrous!
Glimmering! Blazing!
Enchanting! Amazing!

Light.

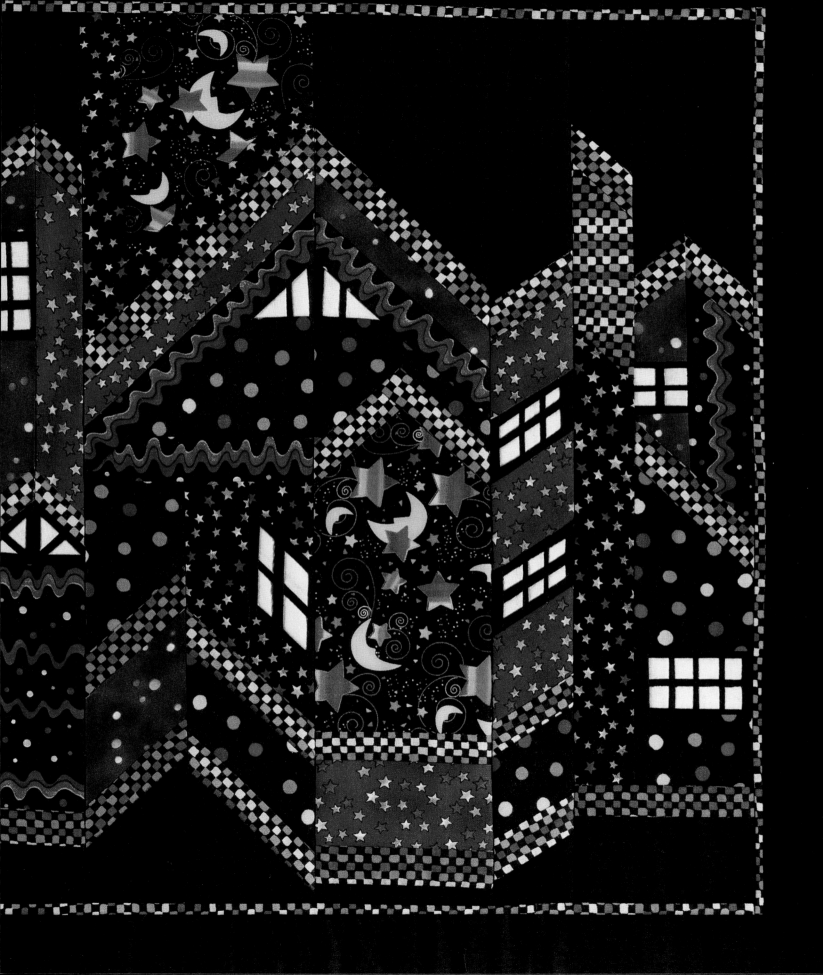

Fireplace

Elf-like,
flames flit
on crimson logs.

One
Little
Candle

One little candle,
a flickering light,
prancing and playing,
pushing back the night.

A hop-skipping flame
putting on a show,
mighty little candle
sets the room aglow.

Protest

Oh, no!
Not fair!
How can this be?
The sun tires out
so long before me.

Lights Out

I pull the covers
over my head
and let out a few snores
for good measure . . .
then snap on my flashlight
and open my book.
Now *this* is
reading for pleasure!

Morning Light

Today I wake
while it's still night,
for I am *Lucia*.

I wear a red sash
and gown of white.
Shhh! I *am* Lucia.

I bring coffee
and saffron buns,
for *I* am Lucia!

With a crown of
candles on my head,
I am Lucia,

Queen of Light!

Solstice

December has the longest nights
of any in the year.
In centuries past folks were afraid
the sun would disappear.
They lit grand fires to bring it back
with feasting and good cheer.

Small Miracles

Hanukkah lights,
another each night,
until there are
eight in a row.
Flames romp on their heads,
and I don't go to bed
until they burn
down to their toes.

It's Time

We've been working.
We've been waiting.
We have been
anticipating.
Make it dark,
as dark can be.
It's time to light
our Christmas tree!

Tree

tip
top
wink
red blue
blink yellow
twinkle green
lights bright sparkling
down to the bottom of
our
glorious tree

Christmas Path

Glowing *farolitos*
all along the street.
Flickering *farolitos*,
bright on Christmas Eve.
Lines of *farolitos*
as far as I can see.
So many *farolitos*,

and some were made by me!

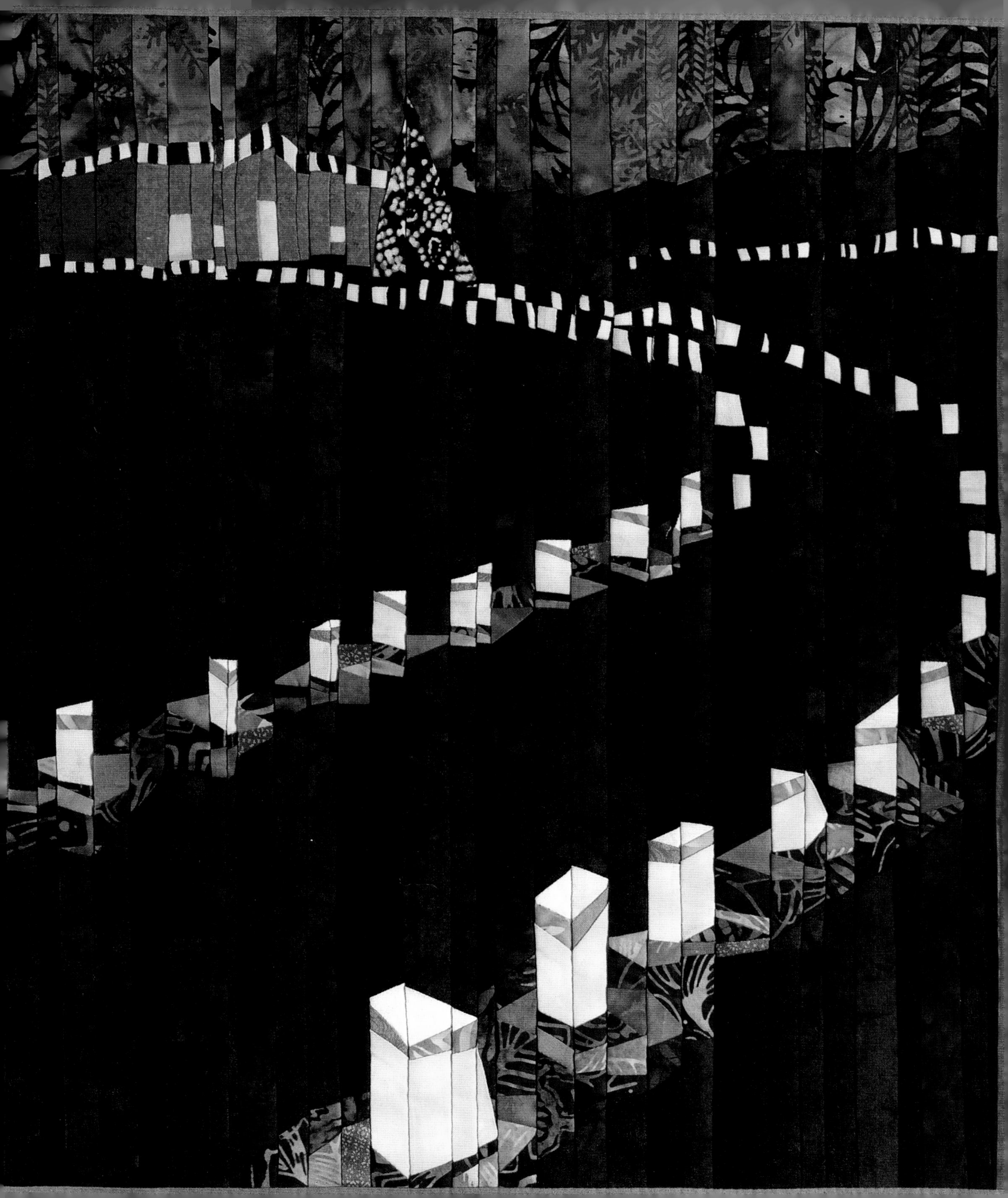

Kwanzaa

Hear the drumbeat.
Light the candles.

Watch the flames skip
to the drumbeat.

Sing the music
of my people.

Feel my feet dance
to the music.

All together
with my family.

Shout "Harambee!"
"Pull together!"

Hear the drumbeat.
See the flames dance.

Sing the music.
Shout "Harambee!"

Nian Is Coming

Nian the monster
has a vast mouth
to gobble us up
in one mammoth bite.

Lurking at New Year,
he waits for his chance.
Hang the red paper
to scare him away.

Stomp with the lions!
Burn the bamboo!
With streamers of fire
we light up the skies!

Wave the red lanterns!
Make a huge noise!
The great, greedy monster
goes hungry this year.

A Sight to See

Aurora borealis!
Aurora borealis!
The words ring out
in a joyful shout.
Come see!

Come see
this amazing sight,
the shifting colors,
a billowing curtain
of swirling,
swooping light.

Aurora borealis!
Aurora borealis!
The words slip out
in a whisper.

Wow.

Artist

Bright as a lightbulb,
round as pie,
the moon glows full
in the winter sky.
It's high overhead,
but far below
the moon paints pictures
on the blue-white snow.

Making the Winter Lights Quilts

During the dark months, we turn to light—a dancing candle, a cozy fire—for comfort and to lift our spirits. Even natural lights have a special quality in winter: the morning sun glinting on icicles, early sunsets, stars glittering in the cold, moonlight on fresh snowfall. For some the most cheerful of all may be the lights we use in winter celebrations.

Thousands of years ago, people didn't understand how the rotation of the earth and its orbit around the sun caused the winter months to grow darker and colder. They feared the sun would disappear altogether. In many cultures, people celebrated midwinter solstice rituals to encourage the return of the sun and its life-giving light. Such rituals were celebrated on every continent and usually involved feasting, merrymaking, gift giving, and decorating with evergreens as symbols of sustained life. They centered around fire and light of some sort, including Yule logs, bonfires, lighted trees, candles, and fireworks.

Many of our winter celebrations today incorporate these same symbols. In Scandinavian traditions, winter holidays begin with Santa Lucia Feast Day, when eldest daughters appear in candlelit crowns. Hanukkah, the Jewish festival of lights, is celebrated with eight days of candle lighting. The evergreen Christmas tree is well-lit to celebrate the birth of Jesus, and *farolitos*, paper bag lanterns, symbolically light the path for Mary and Joseph in much of the southwestern United States. Chinese New Year celebrations include fireworks to frighten off bad spirits, including *Nian*, the monster who threatens at the end of the old year. Kwanzaa celebrates the rich heritage, abilities, and hopes of African Americans with seven days of candle lighting.

The lights of winter—breathtaking natural light, warm cozy indoor light, high-spirited holiday lights—are all the more striking because of the cold and darkness that surround them. The contrast of dark and light, warm and cold, is what makes the lights so appealing, and I needed to capture these contrasts in the images for this book. Quilts, warm cozy quilts, seemed to be the perfect medium to express the comforting quality of winter light. I had often admired quilts that seemed to glow and was excited by the challenge of creating some of my own. But how?

The rather obvious secret to making colors glow is to surround bright luminous colors with intense dark ones. The stronger the contrast between them, the more the bright shades appear to light up. Since light so often seems to swirl in the air or dance across surfaces, movement was another ingredient I wanted in these quilts. The appearance of movement can be created by using pieces with diagonal rather than horizontal and vertical lines. I had to search for the perfect fabrics—and some new techniques for quiltmaking.

TWISTED LOG CABIN

In a traditional Log Cabin quilt block, strips of light and dark fabric make the "walls" of the cabin, surrounding the center square "hearth." The result is a set of concentric squares. As in many quilt patterns, the name is symbolic, describing the way it is constructed, not the way it looks.

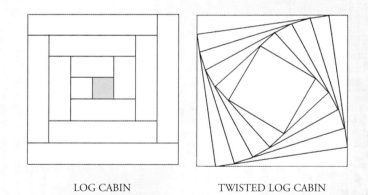

LOG CABIN   TWISTED LOG CABIN

The Twisted Log Cabin is created by doing just that, twisting each concentric square, beginning from the outside into the center square. In this way, the appearance of movement is created in a single quilt block, and, when combined with other blocks, that movement can really seem to twist and swirl. This technique can also be used with other geometric shapes. With their angled sides, triangles and parallelograms can give the sense of even more movement.

For my twisted triangles, I made sets of graduating colors of fabric that I sewed in precise order onto the small triangle pattern that I printed in sheets from my computer. Each triangle is 1⅜" on a side and is made up of 13 smaller triangles.

To be sure each color was sewn in the right place, I marked the back of each triangle with fabric markers. I sewed the triangles into strips, then sewed the strips together.

The back of the "Solstice" quilt shows the pieced triangles and innumerable stitches.

Both "Solstice" and "Star Catcher" are constructed with 650 of these pieced triangles, each of which is made up of 13 insanely small triangles—for a grand total of 8,450 triangles per quilt! I spent about four hundred hours sewing the "Solstice" quilt, but there was a lot of learning, ripping, and resewing in the process. I was sure "Star Catcher," the last quilt I made, would go faster. I was wrong. Capturing the gradual color change of the background proved to be a whole new challenge. "Star Catcher" also took about four hundred hours.

"Fireplace" and "One Little Candle" were similarly challenging, but made with slightly larger triangles and parallelograms. "Lights Out" is the same technique but uses only two large hexagons as the base, making it much easier.

STRIP PIECING

In strip piecing, a design or picture is created by sewing various colors of fabric into strips, then sewing the strips in parallel rows onto a backing. Careful choice and placement of the colors produce images such as the candlelit bags and patterns of light in "Christmas Path" and the Menorah, star, and dreidel in "Small Miracles." The strips also allow for interesting variation in the backgrounds. The contrast between the vertical lines of the backgrounds and the angled lines of the flames, halos, and shadows makes the flames and light seem to move in these quilts.

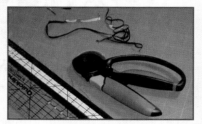

I sewed the fabric to strips of paper on which I had traced my design, then trimmed each side, allowing a quarter inch of fabric for the seam.

Placing the new strip onto the quilt facedown with edges matching, I sewed it along the edge of the paper, through both strips, the flannel batting, and backing fabric. In this way the quilting is done (through all the layers of fabric) as the top layer is sewn, or pieced, together.

"Holiday Magic" uses much wider strips. The windows were pieced together before being sewn into the strips. "It's Time"/"Tree" is done with a variation of strip piecing; in this case the strips are not parallel and were sewn in four sections, then sewn together to make the complete quilt top. After piecing the top in this way, I layered it with cotton padding and backing fabric and quilted by hand through all three layers.

BARGELLO

Bargello is a special type of strip piecing based on traditional needlework patterns in which colors are staggered up and down in vertical rows to form a design resembling flames— lots of movement! It seemed a natural for

the flowing aurora borealis in "A Sight to See," for the radiating light of "Morning Light," and for the monster and fireworks in "Nian Is Coming," too. For these quilts I cut fabric into strips and sewed them together to make a large block. I then cut across these sewn-together strips to make new strips consisting of patches of each of the fabrics. I arranged these strips so that the colors moved up or down to make the pattern in the finished quilt.

Following the design I'd created on my computer, I sewed long strips of fabric together to make a striped block.

I then cut across the block to make new strips of fabric that I arranged to create the staggered design.

APPLIQUÉ

In this technique, which is the only one I have used extensively before, layers of fabric are sewn one on top of the other to create the finished picture. A lot of the movement in these quilts is created by the fabrics themselves. The sky fabric in the "Protest" and "Artist" quilts was painted by Mickey Lawler of Skydyes™. "Kwanzaa" is done with figures appliquéd onto a base made by sewing blocks of African fabrics together.

The first time I proposed illustrating a picture book with quilts, my editor Susan Hirschman said I was crazy. I did it anyway, not just once but twice . . . and now I've done it a third time. Of the three, *Winter Lights* has been by far the most challenging.

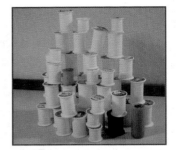

Empty thread spools

The quilts for this book turned out to be much more complicated and time-consuming than I expected, particularly those done with the tiny twisted triangles. The finished quilts, including borders, are 31 by 19 inches—about twice as big as this book—so the pieces are very small. It took almost two and a half years and eleven and a half miles of thread to complete all fifteen quilts. This time, even *I* think I'm crazy . . . but I'm not sorry.

My trash is quite colorful, with snippets of fabric and thread trimmings.

For more information about the holidays, quilting, and quilting activities for all ages, please see my website, www.aghines.com.

Acknowledgments: I was inspired by *Log Cabin with a Twist*, by Barbara T. Kaempfer, American Quilter Society, 1995, and Marge Edie's books *Bargello Quilts* (1994) and *A New Slant on Bargello Quilts* (1998), both published by Martingale.

For Timmie, who knows about light

The handmade quilts used as illustrations in this book were reproduced in full color. The text type is Belwe Medium.
Library of Congress Cataloging-in-Publication Data. Hines, Anna Grossnickle. Winter lights: a season in poems and quilts / by Anna Grossnickle Hines.   p.   cm.
"Greenwillow Books." ISBN 0-06-000817-2 (trade). ISBN 0-06-000818-0 (lib. bdg.). 1. Winter—Juvenile poetry. 2. Children's poetry, American. I. Title.
PS3558.I528W56 2005 811'.54—dc22 2004010869

First Edition 10 9 8 7 6 5 4 3 2 1   Greenwillow Books